All About Mom and Me

WOMEN Weekly
TOP
COMICS
No 6
MOVIE TICKET
TICKET

all about MOM and ME

A Journal for Mothers and Sons

Illustrations by Amir Abou-Roumié

ROCKRIDGE PRESS

First Rockridge Press hardcover edition 2022

Originally published in trade paperback by Rockridge Press 2022

For general information on our other products and services, please contact our Customer Care Department within the United States at (866) 744-2665, or outside the United States at (510) 253-0500.

Hardcover ISBN: 979-8-88608-591-4
Paperback ISBN: 978-1-63807-980-4

Manufactured in the United States of America

Series Designer: Lindsey Dekker
Interior and Cover Designer: Jennifer Hsu
Art Producer: Melissa Malinowsky
Editor: Jesse Aylen
Production Editor: Holland Baker
Production Manager: Riley Hoffman

10 9 8 7 6 5 4 3 2 1 0

This journal belongs to:

MOTHER

and

SON

Getting on the Same Page

Welcome to *All About Mom and Me: A Journal for Mothers and Sons*! From sharing embarrassing moments to describing your perfect day, this journal is an opportunity for the two of you as mother and son to learn more about each other in a fun and creative way. For the sons, maybe you'll find out that your mom also hated broccoli as a kid. For the moms, perhaps you'll be pleasantly surprised to discover that your son's favorite memory is not what you would have guessed.

Before you begin writing, consider sitting down to talk about how exactly this process will work. To make it easier, you'll find some guidelines that you can discuss together. If you just can't wait to start writing, it's okay to skip all that and jump right in! The "right" way to use this journal is whatever works best for the two of you.

Is This a Secret?

Something you may want to talk about is who else, if anyone, will be allowed to see this journal. If you decide it's just for the two of you, then you may need to brainstorm a great hiding spot to keep it safe from nosy family members and friends!

Speaking of nosy family members and friends, will you allow each other to talk about the journal with anyone else? Or will you pinky-swear that it'll be a mother-son secret forever? It's important that you both agree on this particular point—otherwise, there may be trouble if a curious aunt, cousin, or close family friend mentions it over a holiday gathering or birthday dinner.

Filling Out Entries

What about filling out the entries themselves? Perhaps one of you is systematic and organized and would naturally fill out the journal in order, and the other is more spontaneous and creative and would like to write about whatever topic seems appealing at the moment. Does one of you choose the prompt on odd days and the other on even days? Discuss the best way to handle this so that you are both (literally!) on the same page.

Passing the Journal Back and Forth

You may also want to discuss how the journal will be passed back and forth. If the journal is being kept top secret, do you have different nightly drop locations and code names, like your own mother-son spy movie? Or will you simply leave it on each other's nightstands when you are done? Find a way that makes the most sense for both of you. If one of you is traveling somewhere or you live in different places from each other, get creative with how you'll pass it between yourselves. You could write in it either when you spend time together, or hand it off during the times when you're apart so that each of you has some time to spend with your entries! Do whatever works best for both of you.

Setting a Schedule

Finally, talk about timing. Will you write in the journal every day? Once a week? Twice a week? Once the journal is passed to the other person, will there be a certain amount of time before they have to return it? Or maybe it will be totally flexible. Some days will be busier than others, and some days you just may not feel like writing at all. That's okay. Think of the journal as a marathon, not a sprint. This is a keepsake you'll have for many years, so taking care and time with it will only make it more valuable for both of you.

Keep in Mind

Now that you've set some guidelines for how to use the journal, here are some ideas to keep in mind when writing your entries.

Be Honest

Remember, this journal is a safe space in which to share your feelings. Maybe there's something you've been wanting to talk about but have been afraid to. The purpose of this experience is to develop a deeper understanding of each other, and being honest with your words and feelings is the best way to do that. Keeping an open mind when using this journal will ensure that both of you feel respected.

Listen to Each Other

There is an opportunity here to really listen to each other. With our everyday schedules, we aren't always able to give people our full attention at the exact moment they want it. We all get busy, whether it's doing homework, making dinner, or finishing chores, and that's totally understandable. But when you hand each other something you've written, think of it as a signal to take a moment (when you can!) to read it and to pay attention to what the other person has to say. If there's one thing that moms and sons have in common, it's that they both want to feel heard.

Have Fun

Above all else, this journal should be a fun activity for the two of you to share. Don't be afraid to be silly or creative or think outside the box. In the drawing section, some of you moms might find out that your artistic abilities peaked at around the fourth grade. Some of you sons might find out drawing is your new favorite creative hobby! One of you might like to be wildly colorful, and the other one might be into black-and-white scribbles. That's okay! No matter how you each express yourself, it's being the "true you" that is most important. Sharing this space should never feel like a "have-to"—if there are times when one of you is just not feeling it, then step away for a while. Don't worry, the journal won't be offended, and it will still be there when you are inspired to write again.

Tell Stories

Every family has its stories . . . some are funny, some are sad, some might make you howl until you've got tears running down your cheeks, and some are bound to be a little bit embarrassing. No matter what you get out of each story, enjoy the telling and learn from it together. Sharing stories provides entertainment, unites us as mothers and sons, and gives us a deeper understanding of our past, our hopes, and what we want for our futures. This journal's prompts will make it easy to transfer those stories from your memory to the page, where they can be relived over and over for many years to come.

★ Mother ★

Describe three things you admire about your son.

1

2

3

★ Son ★

Describe three things you admire about your mom.

1

2

3

★ Mother ★

What is your favorite season?

What are four things you like about that time of year?

1

2

3

4

★ Son ★

What is your favorite season?

What are four things you like about that time of year?

1

2

3

4

★ Mother ★

Did you have a favorite pet as a child? If you didn't have a pet, what pet would you choose if you could have had one and why?

Do you have any stories about this pet?

★ Son ★

Do you have any pets? If yes, do you want any other pets? If no, do you want a pet?

What is your favorite thing about your pet? If you don't have a pet, what pet would you choose if you could have one and why?

Mother

What's the nicest thing a friend has ever done for you?

What's the nicest thing you've ever done for a friend?

★ Son ★

What's the nicest thing a friend has ever done for you?

What's the nicest thing you've ever done for a friend?

★ Mother ★

What would you do if you could trade places with your son for a day?

★ Son ★

What would you do if you could trade places with your mom for a day?

★ Mother ★

If you could rule the world for a day, what exactly would you do?

★ Son ★

If you could rule the world for a day, what exactly would you do?

★ Mother ★

In what ways are you most similar to your son?

In what ways are you most different?

★ Son ★

How are you and your mom alike?

How are you and your mom different?

★ Mother ★

What was your very first job? How much did you get paid?

What did you learn from this job?

★ Son ★

If you could get a job right now, what would you want to do?

What would you do with the money you made?

★ Mother ★

Who is the person you find it easiest to talk to? Why did you choose this person?

Whom do you trust the most?

★ Son ★

Who is the person you find it easiest to talk to? Why did you choose this person?

Whom do you trust the most?

Who is the person you would trust the most with a secret?

Mother

What is the best gift you've ever received?

What is the best gift you've ever given someone?

★ Son ★

What is the best gift you've ever received?

What is the best gift you've ever given someone?

Mother

Describe your son in five words.

1 ______________________

2 ______________________

3 ______________________

4 ______________________

5 ______________________

Describe yourself in five words.

1 ______________________

2 ______________________

3 ______________________

4 ______________________

5 ______________________

★ Son ★

Describe your mom in five words.

1 ______

2 ______

3 ______

4 ______

5 ______

Describe yourself in five words.

1 ______

2 ______

3 ______

4 ______

5 ______

★ Mother ★

Who is your favorite TV family?

What are the qualities you admire about them?

★ Son ★

Who is your favorite TV family?

Do you think it would be fun to be a part of this family? Why or why not?

★ Mother ★

Who was your favorite teacher as a child? Why?

What was your favorite subject in school?

What was your least favorite subject in school?

★ Son ★

Who is your favorite teacher?

What is the best thing about this teacher?

What is your favorite subject in school?

What is your least favorite subject in school?

★ Mother ★

Things that make you laugh:

Things that make you cry:

Things that make you proud:

Things that make you excited:

★ Son ★

Things that make you laugh:

Things that make you cry:

Things that make you proud:

Things that make you excited:

Mother

What was your favorite vacation as a child?

Whom did you go with, and what did you do there?

Son

What is the best vacation you've been on?

If you could pick any vacation spot, where would it be?

Whom would you bring on vacation with you?

Mother

What is the best thing about your family?

What is the most unusual thing about your family?

★ Son ★

What is the best thing about your family?

What is the most unusual thing about your family?

★ Mother ★

Draw a portrait of your son:

★ Son ★

Draw a portrait of your mom:

★ Mother ★

Tell a story about a time you got in trouble.

What did you learn from that experience?

★ Son ★

Tell a story about a time you got in trouble.

What did you learn from that experience?

★ Mother ★

What is your favorite holiday?

What are three reasons why this holiday is your favorite?

1

2

3

What is your favorite memory of this holiday?

★ Son ★

What is your favorite holiday?

What are three reasons why this holiday is your favorite?

1

2

3

What is your favorite memory of this holiday?

★ Mother ★

What was your most embarrassing moment as a child?

When were you most proud of yourself as a child?

★ Son ★

What was your most embarrassing moment?

What was your proudest moment?

★ Mother ★

If you could have any superpower, what would it be?

How would you use it to make the world a better place?

★ Son ★

If you could have any superpower, what would it be?

How would you use it to make the world a better place?

★ Mother ★

How did you spend your summer days as a child?

What things did you do that your son has not yet experienced?

★ Son ★

What's your favorite thing about summer?

What's one way your summer could be better?

Mother

What is your favorite breakfast?

What is your favorite kind of cookie?

What is one food you never get tired of?

What is the most unusual food you've ever eaten?

What is one food you never want to eat again?

Son

What is your favorite breakfast?

What is your favorite kind of cookie?

What is one food you never get tired of?

What is the most unusual food you've ever eaten?

What is one food you never want to eat again?

★ Mother ★

Describe a perfect day with your son.

★ Son ★

If you could plan a perfect day with your mom, where would you go, and what would you do?

★ Mother ★

What is your favorite birthday memory?

What is the worst birthday gift you've ever received?

Have you ever had a surprise party? If not, would you want one? If so, share about it.

★ Son ★

What is your favorite birthday memory?

What is the worst birthday gift you've ever received?

Have you ever had a surprise party? If not, would you want one? If so, share about it.

Mother

What is an outdoor activity you'd like to do with your son?

Make plans to do it together! Afterward, share your thoughts on how it went. What did you enjoy about it?

★ Son ★

What is an outdoor activity you'd like to do with your mom?

Make plans to do it together! Afterward, share your thoughts on how it went. What did you enjoy about it?

★ Mother ★

What is the best advice your parents ever gave you?

If you could make your son follow one piece of advice, what would it be?

★ Son ★

What is the best advice your mom ever gave you?

If you could give your mom one piece of advice, what would it be?

★ Mother ★

Who is a leader who inspires you?

What are the qualities that a leader should have?

★ Son ★

Who is a leader who inspires you?

Would you want to be a leader? Why or why not?

★ Mother ★

You won the lottery! Draw how you would spend your money:

★ Son ★

You won the lottery! Draw how you would spend your money:

Mother

What did you eat for breakfast as a child?

Did you bring lunch to school, or did you buy lunch in the cafeteria?

What was the best thing your parents made for dinner?

★ Son ★

What foods do you usually eat for breakfast?

Would you rather bring your lunch from home or buy it at school?

What's your favorite thing your mom makes for dinner?

★ Mother ★

What is the best place you've ever been?

What are three reasons that this place is special?

1

2

3

★ Son ★

What is the best place you've ever been?

What are three reasons that this place is special?

1

2

3

★ Mother ★

What is one place you would like to go with your son?

★ Son ★

What is one place you would like to go with your mom?

★ Mother ★

When do you feel the strongest?

When do you feel the weakest?

Son

When do you feel the strongest?

When do you feel the weakest?

★ Mother ★

Did you fight with your siblings or other family members growing up? If so, what did you fight about?

Did you like being the only/oldest/middle/youngest child? Why?

★ Son ★

Do you fight with your siblings or other family members? If so, what do you fight about the most?

Do you like being the only/oldest/middle/youngest child? Why?

★ Mother ★

What is your greatest talent?

What are some talents you wish you had?

★ Son ★

What is your greatest talent?

What are some talents you wish you had?

★ Mother ★

Did you have a favorite grandparent?

What is something they taught you?

What is your favorite memory involving them?

Son

What is the best thing about your grandparents?

What is one thing your grandparents have taught you?

What is your favorite memory involving your grandparents?

★ Mother ★

What is something your son does that makes you laugh?

____

What's the funniest thing your son has ever said?

____

★ Son ★

What is something your mom does that makes you laugh?

____

What happened that made your mom laugh the most?

____

★ Mother ★

If you could invent one thing, what would it be?

Why do you think this invention is needed?

★ Son ★

If you could invent one thing, what would it be?

Why do you think this invention is needed?

★ Mother ★

What was the hardest age for you growing up?

What do you think would have made this age a little easier for you?

★ Son ★

If you could be any age, what age would you be?

What do you think would be fun about being this age?

★ Mother ★

Have you ever lost a friendship?

Do you regret losing that friendship? Is there something you could have done to fix the friendship?

★ Son ★

Have you ever had a fight with a friend?

How would you handle the situation differently next time?

★ Mother ★

What are three important things your son has taught you?

1 ______________________________

2 ______________________________

3 ______________________________

★ Son ★

What are three important things your mom has taught you?

1 ______________________________

2 ______________________________

3 ______________________________

★ Mother ★

Who is the bravest person you know?

What makes them brave?

Son

Who is the bravest person you know?

What makes them brave?

★ Mother ★

The best part of being a mom is:

The hardest part of being a mom is:

★ Son ★

The best part of being a son is:

The hardest part of being a son is:

★ Mother ★

What was your favorite book as a child?

What was your son's favorite book when he was little?

★ Son ★

What is your favorite book?

If you wrote a book, what would the title be?

★ Mother ★

What famous person would you most like to meet?

How would you spend a day with them?

★ Son ★

What famous person would you most like to meet?

How would you spend a day with them?

★ Mother ★

Draw your dream home:

★ Son ★

Draw your dream home:

★ Mother ★

What language would you like to learn?

How would speaking this language benefit you?

★ Son ★

What language would you like to learn?

How would speaking this language be helpful to you?

★ Mother ★

If you were granted three wishes, what would you wish for?

1 ____________________

2 ____________________

3 ____________________

★ Son ★

If you were granted three wishes, what would you wish for?

1 ____________________

2 ____________________

3 ____________________

Mother

What's the biggest difference between your childhood and your son's childhood?

What are some things that are the same?

★ Son ★

What do you think your mom's childhood was like?

Do you think it was harder or easier than yours? Why?

★ Mother ★

What keeps you up at night worrying?

Why do you think this worries you?

★ Son ★

What is something that worries you?

You would worry less about it if:

★ Mother ★

What has been your greatest accomplishment?

What is something you would like to accomplish in the future?

★ Son ★

What has been your greatest accomplishment so far?

What is something you'd like to accomplish in the future?

★ Mother ★

Who was your best friend when you were your son's age?

What are the qualities you liked most about them?

What is your favorite memory involving them?

★ Son ★

Who is your best friend?

What are the things you like best about them?

What are your favorite things to do together?

★ Mother ★

What did you want to be when you grew up?

How is your life similar to or different from that now?

★ Son ★

What do you want to be when you grow up?

What are some things you can do to achieve this?

Mother

What are three things you wish for your son?

1

2

3

★ Son ★

What are three things you wish for your mom?

1

2

3

Mother

What is something your son doesn't know about you?

Son

What is something you don't think your mom knows about you?

★ Mother ★

What are some toys, books, or keepsakes you saved from your childhood?

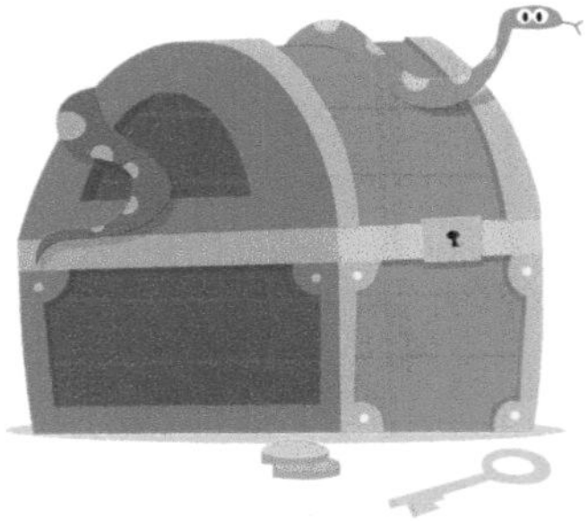

What is your favorite story about one of them?

★ Son ★

What are some things that you want to keep forever?

Why do you want to keep them?

★ Mother ★

What is something that is hard for you to talk about?

What would make it easier for you to open up?

★ Son ★

What is something that is hard for you to talk about?

What would make it easier for you to open up?

★ Mother ★

Draw your future self:

★ Son ★

Draw your future self:

★ Mother ★

What is a rainy day activity you'd like to do with your son?

Make plans to do it together! Afterward, share your thoughts on how it went. What did you enjoy about it?

★ Son ★

What is a rainy day activity you'd like to do with your mom?

Make plans to do it together! Afterward, share your thoughts on how it went. What did you enjoy about it?

★ Mother ★

Were your parents strict when you were growing up?

Did you have to do chores?

Did you get an allowance?

★ Son ★

When is your mom strict?

Are you responsible for any chores? If so, which ones?

Do you think kids should get an allowance? Why or why not?

★ Mother ★

What is the best part of having siblings or cousins?

What were your favorite things to do with your siblings or cousins when you were growing up?

★ Son ★

What is the best part of having siblings or cousins?

What are your favorite things to do with your siblings or cousins?

Mother

Describe what you think your life will be like in 20 years. Where will you be living? How will you spend your days?

What will your son be like in 20 years?

Son

Describe what you think your life will be like in 20 years. Where will you be living? How will you spend your days?

What will your mom be like in 20 years?

★ Mother ★

What are some things you can do to be a helpful member of society?

____

____

____

____

★ Son ★

What are some things you can do to be a helpful member of society?

____

____

____

____

★ Mother ★

What is the best part of being a grown-up?

What is the most challenging part of being a grown-up?

★ Son ★

What is the best part of being a kid?

What is the most challenging part of being a kid?

★ Mother ★

If you could travel back in time to one year in your life, which year would it be?

What would you do differently during that year?

★ Son ★

If you could relive one day of your life over again, which day would it be?

What is something you would do differently on that day, and why?

★ Mother ★

What do you think your son's most prized possession is?

What is your most prized possession?

★ Son ★

What do you think your mom's most prized possession is?

What is your most prized possession?

★ Mother ★

Who is your favorite singer/band?

What are some of your favorite songs?

What was the best concert you've ever been to?

Who is an artist your son likes but you don't?

★ Son ★

Who is your favorite singer/band?

What are some of your favorite songs?

If you could go to any concert, what would it be?

Who is a singer you like but your mom doesn't?

Mother

What are some qualities you admire most in other people?

What qualities do you think people admire about you?

Son

What are some qualities you admire most in other people?

What qualities do you think people admire about you?

★ Mother ★

What is the best thing about the country you live in?

What is a law that you would change?

★ Son ★

What is the best thing about the country you live in?

What is a law that you would change?

★ Mother ★

What was the coolest technology you had when you were a child?

What is your favorite technology today?

★ Son ★

What do you think is the coolest technology now?

What do you think technology will be like when you reach your mom's age?

Mother

What makes you sad?

What comforts you when you're sad?

Son

What makes you sad?

What comforts you when you're sad?

★ Mother ★

Who is the funniest person you know?

Who is the most generous person you know?

Who is the most hardworking person you know?

Whom can you always count on?

Whom do you argue with the most?

★ Son ★

Who is the funniest person you know?

Who is the most generous person you know?

Who is the most hardworking person you know?

Whom can you always count on?

Whom do you argue with the most?

★ Mother ★

What was your favorite sport or game to play as a child?

What did you like about it?

What is your favorite sport or game now?

★ Son ★

What is your favorite sport or game?

What are some reasons you like to play it?

What is a sport or game you'd like to learn?

Mother

Why did your parents choose your name?

If you could choose your own name, what would it be?

Son

Why did your parents choose your name?

If you could choose a name for yourself, what would it be?

If you have a child someday, what will you name them?

★ Mother ★

If you were stranded on a desert island, which three people would you want with you?

How would these people make your experience on the island easier or better?

★ Son ★

If you were stranded on a desert island, which three people would you want with you?

How would these people make your experience on the island easier or better?

★ Mother ★

You have been invited to a fancy party. Design an outfit to wear:

★ Son ★

You have been invited to a fancy party. Design an outfit to wear:

★ Mother ★

What about your childhood are you most grateful for?

What is something you wish had been different?

★ Son ★

What are three things you are grateful for?

1

2

3

What is something you wish was different about your life?

★ Mother ★

What is the most important thing you learned in school?

What are some ways that education can be improved?

Son

What is the most important thing you've learned in school?

What are some ways that you think your education could be improved?

★ Mother ★

What would a fun mother-son bonding night look like? What activities would you do?

Make plans to do it together! Afterward, share your thoughts on how it went. What was your favorite part?

★ Son ★

What would a fun mother-son bonding night look like? What activities would you do?

Make plans to do it together! Afterward, share your thoughts on how it went. What was your favorite part?

★ Mother ★

What are three places you'd like to travel to, and why?

1

2

3

★ Son ★

What are three places you'd like to travel to, and why?

1

2

3

Mother

When were you most proud of your son?

★ Son ★

When was your mom most proud of you?